HAL•LEONARD
INSTRUMENTAL
PLAY-ALONG

AUDIO
ACCESS
INCLUDED

VIOLA

BEST OF METALLICA

T0068450

PLAYBACK+
Speed • Pitch • Balance • Loop

To access audio visit:
www.halleonard.com/mylibrary

2338-9166-5743-2287

Recorded by Scott Seelig

Cherry Lane Music Company
Educational Director/Project Supervisor: Susan Poliniak
Director of Publications: Mark Phillips
Publications Coordinator: Rebecca Skidmore

ISBN: 978-1-60378-122-0

Visit Hal Leonard Online at
www.halleonard.com

CONTENTS

The Day That Never Comes

Music by Metallica
Lyrics by James Hetfield

VIOLA

Enter Sandman

Words and Music by
James Hetfield, Lars Ulrich and Kirk Hammett

VIOLA

Fade to Black

Words and Music by
James Hetfield, Lars Ulrich,
Cliff Burton and Kirk Hammett

VIOLA

Harvester of Sorrow

Words and Music by
James Hetfield and Lars Ulrich

VIOLA

Nothing Else Matters

Words and Music by
James Hetfield and Lars Ulrich

VIOLA

One

Words and Music by
James Hetfield and Lars Ulrich

Sad but True

Words and Music by
James Hetfield and Lars Ulrich

VIOLA

Seek & Destroy

Words and Music by
James Hetfield and Lars Ulrich

VIOLA

The Thing That Should Not Be

Words and Music by
James Hetfield, Lars Ulrich and Kirk Hammett

VIOLA

Medium Rock

The Unforgiven

Words and Music by
James Hetfield, Lars Ulrich and Kirk Hammett

VIOLA

Until It Sleeps

Words and Music by
James Hetfield and Lars Ulrich

VIOLA

Welcome Home (Sanitarium)

Words and Music by
James Hetfield, Lars Ulrich and Kirk Hammett

VIOLA

HAL·LEONARD INSTRUMENTAL PLAY-ALONG

Your favorite songs are arranged just for solo instrumentalists with this outstanding series. Each book includes great full-accompaniment play-along audio so you can sound just like a pro! Check out www.halleonard.com to see all the titles available.

12 Hot Singles

Broken (lovelytheband) • Havana (Camila Cabello) • Heaven (Kane Brown) • High Hopes (Panic! At the Disco) • The Middle (Zedd, Maren Morris & Grey) • Natural (Imagine Dragons) • No Place like You (Backstreet Boys) • Shallow (Lady Gaga & Bradley Cooper) • Sucker (Jonas Brothers) • Sunflower (Post Malone & Swae Lee) • thank u, next (Ariana Grande) • Youngblood (5 Seconds of Summer).

____ 00298576 Flute $14.99
____ 00298577 Clarinet.......... $14.99
____ 00298578 Alto Sax.......... $14.99
____ 00298579 Tenor Sax $14.99
____ 00298580 Trumpet $14.99
____ 00298581 Horn $14.99
____ 00298582 Trombone........ $14.99
____ 00298583 Violin............ $14.99
____ 00298584 Viola $14.99
____ 00298585 Cello $14.99

12 Pop Hits

Believer • Can't Stop the Feeling • Despacito • It Ain't Me • Look What You Made Me Do • Million Reasons • Perfect • Send My Love (To Your New Lover) • Shape of You • Slow Hands • Too Good at Goodbyes • What About Us.

____ 00261790 Flute $12.99
____ 00261791 Clarinet.......... $12.99
____ 00261792 Alto Sax.......... $12.99
____ 00261793 Tenor Sax $12.99
____ 00261794 Trumpet $12.99
____ 00261795 Horn $12.99
____ 00261796 Trombone........ $12.99
____ 00261797 Violin............ $12.99
____ 00261798 Viola $12.99
____ 00261799 Cello $12.99

Classic Rock

Don't Fear the Reaper • Fortunate Son • Free Fallin' • Go Your Own Way • Jack and Diane • Money • Old Time Rock & Roll • Sweet Home Alabama • 25 or 6 to 4 • and more.

____ 00294356 Flute $14.99
____ 00294357 Clarinet.......... $14.99
____ 00294358 Alto Sax.......... $14.99
____ 00294359 Tenor Sax $14.99
____ 00294360 Trumpet $14.99
____ 00294361 Horn $14.99
____ 00294362 Trombone........ $14.99
____ 00294363 Violin............ $14.99
____ 00294364 Viola $14.99
____ 00294365 Cello $14.99

Contemporary Broadway

Defying Gravity (from Wicked) • Michael in the Bathroom (from Be More Chill) • My Shot (from Hamilton) • Seize the Day (from Newsies) • She Used to Be Mine (from Waitress) • Stupid with Love (from Mean Girls) • Waving Through a Window (from Dear Evan Hansen) • When I Grow Up (from Matilda) • and more.

____ 00298704 Flute $14.99
____ 00298705 Clarinet.......... $14.99
____ 00298706 Alto Sax.......... $14.99
____ 00298707 Tenor Sax $14.99
____ 00298708 Trumpet $14.99
____ 00298709 Horn $14.99
____ 00298710 Trombone........ $14.99
____ 00298711 Violin............ $14.99
____ 00298712 Viola $14.99
____ 00298713 Cello $14.99

Disney Movie Hits

Beauty and the Beast • Belle • Circle of Life • Cruella De Vil • Go the Distance • God Help the Outcasts • Hakuna Matata • If I Didn't Have You • Kiss the Girl • Prince Ali • When She Loved Me • A Whole New World.

____ 00841420 Flute $12.99
____ 00841421 Clarinet.......... $12.99
____ 00841422 Alto Sax.......... $12.99
____ 00841423 Trumpet $12.99
____ 00841424 French Horn $12.99
____ 00841425 Trombone/Baritone $12.99
____ 00841426 Violin............ $12.99
____ 00841427 Viola $12.99
____ 00841428 Cello $12.99
____ 00841686 Tenor Sax $12.99
____ 00841687 Oboe $12.99

Disney Solos

Be Our Guest • Can You Feel the Love Tonight • Colors of the Wind • Friend like Me • Part of Your World • Under the Sea • You'll Be in My Heart • You've Got a Friend in Me • Zero to Hero • and more.

____ 00841404 Flute $12.99
____ 00841405 Clarinet/Tenor Sax . $12.99
____ 00841406 Alto Sax.......... $12.99
____ 00841407 Horn $12.99
____ 00841408 Trombone/Baritone $12.99
____ 00841409 Trumpet $12.99
____ 00841410 Violin............ $12.99
____ 00841411 Viola $12.99
____ 00841412 Cello $12.99
____ 00841506 Oboe $12.99
____ 00841553 Mallet Percussion .. $12.99

Great Classical Themes

Blue Danube Waltz (Strauss) • Can Can (from Orpheus in the Underworld) (Offenbach) • Jesu, Joy of Man's Desiring (J.S. Bach) • Morning Mood (from Peer Gynt) (Grieg) • Ode to Joy (from Symphony No. 9) (Beethoven) • William Tell Overture (Rossini) • and more.

____ 00292727 Flute $12.99
____ 00292728 Clarinet.......... $12.99
____ 00292729 Alto Sax.......... $12.99
____ 00292730 Tenor Sax $12.99
____ 00292732 Trumpet $12.99
____ 00292733 Horn $12.99
____ 00292735 Trombone........ $12.99
____ 00292736 Violin............ $12.99
____ 00292737 Viola $12.99
____ 00292738 Cello $12.99

The Greatest Showman

Come Alive • From Now On • The Greatest Show • A Million Dreams • Never Enough • The Other Side • Rewrite the Stars • This Is Me • Tightrope.

____ 00277389 Flute $14.99
____ 00277390 Clarinet.......... $14.99
____ 00277391 Alto Sax.......... $14.99
____ 00277392 Tenor Sax $14.99
____ 00277393 Trumpet $14.99
____ 00277394 Horn $14.99
____ 00277395 Trombone........ $14.99
____ 00277396 Violin............ $14.99
____ 00277397 Viola $14.99
____ 00277398 Cello $14.99

Irish Favorites

Danny Boy • I Once Loved a Lass • The Little Beggarman • The Minstrel Boy • My Wild Irish Rose • The Wearing of the Green • and dozens more!

____ 00842489 Flute $12.99
____ 00842490 Clarinet.......... $12.99
____ 00842491 Alto Sax.......... $12.99
____ 00842493 Trumpet $12.99
____ 00842494 Horn $12.99
____ 00842495 Trombone........ $12.99
____ 00842496 Violin............ $12.99
____ 00842497 Viola $12.99
____ 00842498 Cello $12.99

Simple Songs

All of Me • Evermore • Hallelujah • Happy • I Gotta Feeling • I'm Yours • Lava • Rolling in the Deep • Viva la Vida • You Raise Me Up • and more.

____ 00249081 Flute $12.99
____ 00249082 Clarinet.......... $12.99
____ 00249083 Alto Sax.......... $12.99
____ 00249084 Tenor Sax $12.99
____ 00249086 Trumpet $12.99
____ 00249087 Horn $12.99
____ 00249089 Trombone........ $12.99
____ 00249090 Violin............ $12.99
____ 00249091 Viola $12.99
____ 00249092 Cello $12.99
____ 00249093 Oboe $12.99
____ 00249094 Keyboard Percussion $12.99

Stadium Rock

Crazy Train • Don't Stop Believin' • Eye of the Tiger • Havana • Seven Nation Army • Sweet Caroline • We Are the Champions • and more.

____ 00323880 Flute $14.99
____ 00323881 Clarinet.......... $14.99
____ 00323882 Alto Sax.......... $14.99
____ 00323883 Tenor Sax $14.99
____ 00323884 Trumpet $14.99
____ 00323885 Horn $14.99
____ 00323886 Trombone........ $14.99
____ 00323887 Violin............ $14.99
____ 00323888 Viola $14.99
____ 00323889 Cello $14.99

Video Game Music

Angry Birds • Assassin's Creed III • Assassin's Creed Revelations • Battlefield 1942 • Civilization IV (Baba Yetu) • Deltarune (Don't Forget) • Elder Scrolls IV & V • Fallout® 4 • Final Fantasy VII • Full Metal Alchemist (Bratja) (Brothers) • IL-2 Sturmovik: Birds of Prey • Splinter Cell: Conviction • Undertale (Megalovania).

____ 00283877 Flute $12.99
____ 00283878 Clarinet.......... $12.99
____ 00283879 Alto Sax.......... $12.99
____ 00283880 Tenor Sax $12.99
____ 00283882 Trumpet $12.99
____ 00283883 Horn $12.99
____ 00283884 Trombone........ $12.99
____ 00283885 Violin............ $12.99
____ 00283886 Viola $12.99
____ 00283887 Cello $12.99

HAL·LEONARD®

E-Z PLAY® TODAY SERIES

OVER 300 VOLUMES AVAILABLE!

The E-Z Play® Today songbook series is the shortest distance between beginning music and playing fun! Features of this series include:

- full-size books – large 9" x 12" format features easy-to-read, easy-to-play music

- accurate arrangements – simple enough for the beginner, but with authentic-sounding chords and melody lines

- minimum number of page turns

- thousands of songs – an incredible array of favorites, from classical and country to Christmas and contemporary hits

- lyrics – most arrangements include complete song lyrics

- most up-to-date registrations - books in the series contain a general registration guide, as well as individual song rhythm suggestions for today's electronic keyboards and organs